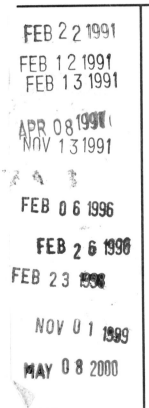

THE MAGIC
OF
BLACK POETRY

Behold, nothing surpasses books.
Would that I might make you love books
   as you do your mother.
Would that I might make their beauty
   enter before your face.
You are to set your heart on books.

EGYPT
Anonymous, c. 2150 B.C.

THE MAGIC
OF
BLACK POETRY

Edited with Commentaries by
RAOUL ABDUL

Illustrations by Dane Burr

DODD, MEAD & COMPANY - NEW YORK

For Aunt Ada & Uncle Ben,
Diane & Denise

The Magic of Black Poetry permissions——

C.3

Thanks are due to the following for permission to reprint the material indicated: Raoul Abdul (translator): for "God," "Call to Prayer," "Humorous Verse," "The Romance of Antar" (adaptation). Samuel Allen: for "To Satch." Russell Atkins: for "Christophe." Broadside Press: for "Booker T. & W. E. B." by Dudley Randall from POEM COUNTERPOEM by Margaret Danner and Dudley Randall, Copyright © 1966 by Dudley Randall. Cambridge University Press: for "The Radish" by Ibn Quzman, "Concert" by Ibn Sharaf from MOORISH POETRY translated by A. J. Arberry, Copyright © 1953 by Cambridge University Press; for "The Moon," "The Sky," "The Sweetest Thing" from AFRICAN POETRY compiled and edited by Ulli Beier, Copyright © 1966 by Cambridge University Press. Clarendon Press, Oxford: for "The Limits of Submission" by Faarah Nuur (pp. 134-136), "Modern Love Song VII" (Anonymous)—English translation only—(pp. 146) from SOMALI POETRY translated by B. W. Adrzejewski and I. M. Lewis, Copyright © 1964 by Oxford University Press. John Pepper Clark: for "Ibadan." Harold Courlander: for "Sunday Morning Song" and "Work Song." Waring Cuney: for "Conception" and "My Lord, What a Morning." Frank Marshall Davis: for excerpt from "Four Glimpses of Night." Owen Dodson: for excerpt from "The Confession Stone." Dodd, Mead & Co.: for "A Negro Love Song," "To a Captious Critic," "Little Brown Baby" from THE COMPLETE POEMS OF PAUL LAURENCE DUNBAR. Doubleday & Co., Inc.: for "Epigram" by Armand Lanusse, "In the Album of Mme—" by Pierre Dalcour (translated by Langston Hughes) from THE POETRY OF THE NEGRO 1746-1970 edited by Arna Bontemps and Langston Hughes, Copyright © 1970 by Arna Bontemps and George Houston Bass, Executors of the Estate of Langston Hughes and Arna Bontemps. Copyright © 1949 by Langston Hughes and Arna Bontemps. Reprinted by permission of Doubleday & Co., Inc. Dorothy Durem: for "Respectful Request." Jaci Earley: for "One Thousand Nine Hundred & Sixty-Eight Winters." James A. Emanuel: for "The Young Ones, Flip Side" by James A. Emanuel from THE NEGRO DIGEST, November 1965, Copyright © 1965 by The Johnson Publishing Co., Inc. Mari Evans: for "The Emancipation of George-Hector" from I AM A BLACK WOMAN by Mari Evans, Copyright © 1970 by Mari Evans. Carol Freeman: for "Christmas Morning, I." Herbert D. Greggs: for "Multi-Colored Balloon." Harper & Row: for the following poems from ON THESE I STAND by Countee Cullen: "For a Poet," Copyright © 1925 by Harper & Row, Publishers, Inc., renewed 1953 by Ida M. Cullen; "For a Lady I Know," Copyright © 1925 by Harper & Row, Publishers, Inc., renewed 1953 by Ida M. Cullen; "For a Mouthy Woman," Copyright © 1925 by Harper & Row, Publishers, Inc., renewed 1953 by Ida M. Cullen; "Christus Natus Est," Copyright © 1947 by Harper & Row, Publishers, Inc.; "Incident," Copyright © 1925 by Harper & Row, Publishers, Inc., renewed 1953 by Ida M. Cullen. By permission of the publishers;

INTRODUCTION

I have wrapped my dreams in a silken cloth,
And laid them away in a box of gold;
Where long will cling the lips of the moth,
I have wrapped my dreams in a silken cloth;
I hide no hate; I am not even wroth
Who found earth's breath so keen and cold;
I have wrapped my dreams in a silken cloth,
And laid them away in a box of gold.

This lovely poem, "*For a Poet,*" was written by the black American poet Countee Cullen. It is the key to this collection of poems by black people from all over the world, from the very beginnings of African time to the present day, especially chosen for young people.

The creation of a poem is an act of magic. The poet is possessed by a remarkable spirit which no one has ever really been able to explain. He has the power to transform a life experience into poetry.

In a sense, the poet wraps his dreams in a silken cloth, and when someone else takes these creations and puts them together in a book, he lays them away in a box of gold.

It is my hope that the reader will browse through the pages of this collection again and again and share with me the magic of black poetry.

Raoul Abdul

CONTENTS

BEGINNINGS

This folk sermon reminds me of the many times I sat in the First Baptist Church in a small town in Canada to hear its minister conjur up magic with words.

GOD

(A Folk Sermon)

I vision God standing
On the heights of heaven,
Throwing the devil like
A burning torch
Over the gulf
Into the valleys of hell.
His eye the lightning's flash,
His voice the thunder's roll.
Wid one hand He snatched
The sun from its socket,
And the other He clapped across the moon.

I vision God wringing
A storm from the heavens;
Rocking the world

Like an earthquake;
Blazing the sea
Wid a trail er fire.
His eye the lightning's flash,
His voice the thunder's roll.
Wid one hand He snatched
The sun from its socket,
And the other He clapped across the moon.

I vision God standing
On a mountain
Of burnished gold,
Blowing His breath
Of silver clouds
Over the world.
His eye the lightning's flash,
His voice the thunder's roll.
Wid one hand He snatched
The sun from its socket,
And the other He clapped across the moon.

U.S.A.

The great Egyptian Pharaoh, Akhenaton, believed that the
Sun was the one and only God.

HYMN TO THE SUN

Pharaoh Akhenaton (c. 1350 B.C.*)*

Beautiful you rise upon the horizon of heaven,
O living sun, you have existed since the beginning of
    things . . .
The whole world is filled with your loveliness.
You are the god Ra, and you have brought every land
    under your yoke,
Bound them in with the force of your love.
You are far away, yet your beams flood down upon the
    earth.
You shine upon the faces of men,
And no one is able to fathom the mystery of your coming.

EGYPT
TRANS: *J. E. Manchip White*

THE MOON

(Oral Traditional)

The moon lights the earth
it lights the earth but still
the night must remain the night.
The night cannot be like the day.
The moon cannot dry our washing.

Just like a woman cannot be a man
Just like black can never be white.

GUINEA
TRANS: *Ulli Beier*

WINTER MOON

Langston Hughes (1902–1967)

How thin and sharp is the moon tonight!
How thin and sharp and ghostly white
Is the slim curved crook of the moon tonight!

U.S.A.

PROPOSITION

Nicolás Guillén (1904–)

Tonight
when the moon comes out
I shall change it
into money.

But I'd be sorry
if people knew about it,
for the moon
is an old family treasure.

CUBA
TRANS: *Langston Hughes*

Poet Saundra Sharp writes: "Moon Poem was written when the astronauts made the first trip to the moon. I was listening to tapes of their broadcast as they gathered samples to bring back to earth, and it sounded rather greedy, which added to my feeling that we had no business going up there in the first place!"

MOON POEM

Saundra Sharp (contemporary)

"Ouu
  gee whiz
  hey charlie
  look
  purple rocks
  hey alan
  over here
  looks like glass
  got to have
  one of these
  just like green glass
  ouu get one of those - - - - "

You'all better leave God's moon alone,
Else he ain't gonna turn it on, no more!

U.S.A.

THE STARS HAVE DEPARTED

Christopher Okigbo (1932–67)

The Stars have departed,
the sky in monocle
surveys the world under.

The stars have departed,
and I—where am I?

Stretch, stretch, O antennae,
to clutch at this hour,
fulfilling each moment in a
broken monody.

NIGERIA

THE SKY

(Oral Traditional)

The sky at night is like a big city
where beasts and men abound,
but never once has anyone killed a fowl or a goat,
and no bear has ever killed a prey.
There are no accidents; there are no losses.
Everything knows its way.

GHANA
TRANS: *Kafu Hoh*

THE CREATION OF MAN

(Adapted from Folk Sermons)

When God said
"I'll make me a man,"
The sun
Gathered up the fiery skirts of her garments
And wheeled around the throne
Saying, "Make man after me!"
God gazed upon the sun
And sent her back to her blood-red socket
And shook his head, "No!"

The moon
Grabbed up the reins of the tides
And dragged a thousand seas behind her
As she walked around the throne
Saying, "Please make man after me!"
But God said "NO!
I'll make man in my own image!"

So God A'mighty
Got His stuff together
He dipped some water out of the mighty deep
He got Him a handful of dirt
From the foundation sills of the earth
He seized a thimble full of breath
From the drums of the wind
And He made man in His own image.

U.S.A.
Adapted from folk material
in *Jonah's Gourd Vine*
by Zora Neale Hurston

SPRINGTIME

IN TIME OF SILVER RAIN

Langston Hughes (1902–1967)

In time of silver rain
The earth
Puts forth new life again,
Green grasses grow
And flowers lift their heads,
And over all the plain
The wonder spreads
    Of life,
    Of life,
    Of life!

In time of silver rain
The butterflies
Lift silken wings
To catch a rainbow cry,
And trees put forth
New leaves to sing
In joy beneath the sky

As down the roadway
Passing boys and girls
Go singing, too,
In time of silver rain
When spring
And life
Are new.

U.S.A.

PLAY SONG

Peter Clarke (contemporary)

Let's go up to the hillside today
to play, to play
to play.

Up to the hill where the daisies grow
Like snow, like snow
like snow.

There shall we make a daisy chain
One tomorrow and tomorrow again
There where the daisies grow like snow
There's where we will go.

Let us go down to the little bay
to play, to play
to play.

Down to the bay where the children swim
    like fish, like fish
    like fish.

Down to the bay where the children swim,
Down to the bay where the white yachts skim,
Or up to the hill where the daisies grow,
There's where we will go.

SOUTH AFRICA

This poem should be acted out. As it is read, you should try to imagine yourself being each one of the characters suggested by the words.

ALL LIVES, ALL DANCES, & ALL IS LOUD
(Oral Traditional)

The fish does . . . HIP
The bird does . . . VISS
The marmot does . . . GNAN

I throw myself to the left,
I turn myself to the right,
I act the fish,
Which darts in the water, which darts

11

Which twists about, which leaps—
All lives, all dances, & all is loud.

The fish does . . . HIP
The bird does . . . VISS
The marmot does . . . GNAN

The bird flies away,
It flies, flies, flies,
Goes, returns, passes,
Climbs, soars & drops.
I act the bird—
All lives, all dances, & all is loud.

The fish does . . . HIP
The bird does . . . VISS
The marmot does . . . GNAN

The monkey from branch to branch,
Runs, bounds & leaps,
With his wife, with his brat,
His mouth full, his tail in the air,
There goes the monkey! There goes the Monkey!
All lives, all dances, & all is loud.

GABON
TRANS: *C. M. Bowra*

THE TWIST

Edward Braithwaite (1930–)

In a little shanty town
was on a night like this

girls were sitting down
around the town
like this

some were young
and some were brown
I even found
a miss

who was black and brown
and really did
the twist

watch her move her wrist
and feel your belly twist
feel the hunger thunder
when her hip bones twist
try to hold her, keep her under
while the juke box hiss
twist the music out of hunger
on a night like this.

BARBADOS

This is a song lyric, so keep the rhythm going steadily when you read this poem.

JUBA DANCE

(Folk Song)

Juba jump and Juba sing,
Juba cut dat pigeon's wing!
Juba kick off Juba's shoe,
Juba dance dat Juba do!
Juba whirl dat foot about,
Juba blow dat candle out!
Juba circle, raise de latch,
Juba do dat Long Dog Scratch!

U.S.A.
Creole

LITTLE SONG FOR THE CHILDREN OF THE ANTILLES

Nicolás Guillén (1904–)

On the sea of the Antilles
floats a boat of paper:
floats and floats the boat boat
with a pilot.

14

From Havana to Portobello,
from Jamaica to Trinidad,
floats and floats the boat boat
without a captain.

A black girl in the stern
and in the prow a Spaniard:
floats and floats the boat boat
with those two.

They pass islands, islands, islands,
many islands, always islands;
floats and floats the boat boat
with stopping.

A chocolate cannon
fires at the boat,
and a cannon of sugar sugar
answers.

Ah, my sailor-boat
with your hull of paper!
Ah, my black and white boat
without a pilot!

There goes the black girl black girl
close close to the Spaniard;
floats and floats the boat boat
with those two.

CUBA
TRANS: *Langston Hughes*

MULTI-COLORED BALLOON

Herbert D. Greggs (1931–)

With my multi-colored balloon
I feel just like I'm under a rainbow;
A blue-green and yellow, red-raspberry jello-y
Funderful rainbow.

I can leap in the air like a silly Pooh Bear,
Or a cow jumping over the moon.
When I'm high in the air
I can spy over there
Where the dish ran away with the spoon.

I can play a squeaky old tune on my colored balloon
If I dare to,
Or dress up like a circus-y clown
With a smile or a frown
Anytime that I care to.

By gosh, oh, by golly
It's fun to be jolly
All laughter this fall afternoon
With my wonderful, funderful
Multi-colored balloon.

U.S.A.

16

THE YOUNG ONES, FLIP SIDE

James A. Emanuel (1921–)

In tight pants, tight skirts,
stretched or squeezed,
youth hurts.
Crammed in, bursting out,
Flesh will sing
And hide its doubt
In nervous hips, hopping glance,
Usurping rouge,
Provoking stance.

Put off, or put on,
Youth hurts. And then
It's gone.

U.S.A.

LOVE

LOVE

(Oral Traditional)

Love is a funny thing
Shaped like a lizard,
Run down your heart strings
And tickle your gizzard.
You can fall from a mountain,
You can fall from above,
But the great fall is
When you fall in love.

U.S.A.

LIFE IN OUR VILLAGE

Matei Markwei (contemporary)

In our little village
When elders are around
Boys must not look at girls
And girls must not look at boys
Because the elders say
That is not good.

Even when night comes
Boys must play separately
Girls must play separately
But humanity is weak
So boys and girls meet.

The boys play hide and seek
And the girls play hide and seek.
The boys know where the girls hide
And the girls know where the boys hide
So in their hide and seek
Boys seek girls
Girls seek boys
And each to each sing
Songs of love.

GHANA

JOY

Langston Hughes (1902–1967)

I went to look for Joy,
Slim, dancing Joy,
Gay, laughing Joy,
Bright-eyed Joy—
And I found her
Driving the butcher's cart
In the arms of the butcher boy!
Such company, such company,
As keeps this young nymph, Joy!

U.S.A.

*This love poem captures the charm of a dialect once widely
spoken in the South. If you read it out loud, you will find that
you must keep a steady beat going because it has a music of
its own.*

A NEGRO LOVE SONG

Paul Laurence Dunbar (1872–1906)

Seen my lady home las' night,
    Jump back, honey, jump back.
Hel' huh han' an' sque'z it tight,
    Jump back, honey, jump back.

Hyeahd huh sigh a little sigh,
Seen a light gleam f'om huh eye,
An' a smile go flittin' by—
    Jump back, honey, jump back.

Hyeahd de win' blow thoo de pine,
    Jump back, honey, jump back.
Mockin'-bird was singin' fine,
    Jump back, honey, jump back.
An' my hea't was beatin' so,
When I reached my lady's do',
Dat I couldn't ba' to go—
    Jump back, honey, jump back.

Put my ahm arooun' huh wais',
    Jump back, honey, jump back.
Raised huh lips an' took a tase,
    Jump back, honey, jump back.
Love me, honey, love me true?
Love me well ez I love you?
An' she answe'd, " 'Cose I do"—
    Jump back, honey, jump back.

U.S.A.

LOVE SONG

(Anonymous)

I passed by the house of the young man who loves me;
I found the door was open.
He sat at his mother's side,
In the midst of his brothers and sisters.
How he stared out at me as I passed by the house!
(I was just strolling by for my own pleasure.)
My heart is on fire with the idea of strolling by again
    tonight
Just to take another peek at my friend . . .

EGYPT
Adapted by *Raoul Abdul*

23

This verse was originally written in French, the language of the Creoles of New Orleans. I like to think of Creoles as Rainbow People because they are a happy mixture of African, French, and Spanish.

VERSE WRITTEN IN THE ALBUM OF MADEMOISELLE—

Pierre Dalcour (c. 1800)

The evening star that in the vaulted skies
Sweetly sparkles, gently flashes,
To me is less lovely than a glance of your eyes
    Beneath their brown lashes.

U.S.A.——CREOLE
TRANS: *Langston Hughes*

SPRING BLOSSOM

Ernest Attah (contemporary)

Shall I compare thee,
Fair creature of an hour,
To a spring blossom,
Bursting forth in lovely splendour?
Or yet shall I,
Thou apple of my eye,

Compare thy charms
To the silvery moon on a summer's eve?

No, I won't—go wash off thy disgusting makeup.

NIGERIA

NONSENSE

DISGRACE
(Oral Traditional)

Pepper and salt,
Vinegar in the face,
Gal, you so ugly
It's a disgrace!

U.S.A.

FOR A LADY I KNOW
Countee Cullen (1903–1946)

She even thinks that up in heaven
    Her class lies late and snores
While poor black cherubs rise at seven
    To do celestial chores.

U.S.A.

27

THE CRAZY WOMAN
Gwendolyn Brooks (1917–)

I shall not sing a May song.
A May song should be gay.
I'll wait until November.
That is the time for me.
I'll go out in the frosty dark
And sing most terribly.

And all the little people
Will stare at me and say,
"That is the Crazy Woman
Who should not sing in May."

U.S.A.

FOR A MOUTHY WOMAN
Countee Cullen (1903–1946)

God and the devil still are wrangling
    Which should have her, which repel;
God wants no discord in his heaven;
    Satan has enough in hell.

U.S.A.

28

Some people are never satisfied no matter what you do for them. But, please don't do what the author suggests in the last verse!

THE LIMITS OF SUBMISSION

Faarah Nuur (c. 1930)

Over and over again to people
I show abundant kindness.

If they are not satisfied
I spread out bedding for them
And invite them to sleep.

If they are still not satisfied,
The milk of the camel whose name is Suub
I milk three times for them,
And tell them to drink it up.

If they are still not satisfied,
I select livestock also
And add them to the tribute.

If they are still not satisfied,
'Oh brother-in-law, oh Sultan, oh King!'
These salutations I lavish upon them.

If they are still not satisfied,
At the time of early morning prayers I prepare

The dark grey horse with black tendons,
And with the words 'Praise to the Prophet' I take
The iron-shafted spear,
And drive it through their ribs
So that their lungs spew out;
Then they are satisfied!

SOMALILAND
TRANS: *B. W. Andrzejewski & I. M. Lewis*

EPIGRAM

Armand Lanusse (1812–67)

"Do you not wish to renounce the Devil?"
Asked a good priest of a woman of evil
Who had so many sins that every year
They cost her endless remorse and fear.
"I wish to renounce him forever," she said,
"But that I may lose every urge to be bad,
Before pure grace takes me in hand,
Shouldn't I show my daughter how to get a man?"

U.S.A.—CREOLE
TRANS: *Langston Hughes*

THE RADISH

Ibn Quzman (d. 1160)

The radish is a good
And doubtless wholesome food,
But proves, to vex the eater,
A powerful repeater.

This only fault I find:
What should be left behind
Comes issuing instead
Right from the eater's head!

MOORISH SPAIN
TRANS: *A. J. Arberry*

MODERN SONG

(Anonymous)

Oh doctor, I have a pain in my heart,
Give me treatment, but don't put me in hospital!

SOMALILAND
TRANS: *B. W. Andrzejewski*
& I. M. Lewis

31

CONCERT

Ibn Sharaf (d. 1068)

Thanks for the lovely time
We spent with you last night;
The music was sublime,
The programme a delight—

The singing of the flies,
Mosquitoes on the flute,
And, as the big surprise,
The fleas that danced to suit.

MOORISH SPAIN
TRANS: *A. J. Arberry*

RESPECTFUL REQUEST

Ray Durem (1915–1963)

Mr. Scientist, is it too late
To make those A-bombs segregate?
One little change would please me fine.
Stamp on them a great big
WHITE ONLY sign!

U.S.A.

Once upon a time the Caliph and his Prime Minister went out hunting gazelles. The Caliph hit one, but the Prime Minister missed and killed a dog instead. This verse was the poet's comment on the event.

HUMOROUS VERSE
Abu Dolama (d. 778)

The Caliph shot a gazelle,
And Ali shot a dog.
Bravo!
Each shall eat the thing he acquired.

ARABIA
TRANS: *Raoul Abdul*

TO A CAPTIOUS CRITIC
Paul Laurence Dunbar (1872–1906)

Dear critic, who my lightness so deplores,
Would I might study to be prince of bores,
Right wisely would I rule that dull estate—
But, sir, I may not, till you abdicate.

U.S.A.

CREATURES

LIZARD

Agnes Maxwell-Hall (1894–)

O, what would people say if you
Ate bitter-tasting ants, drank dew,
Caught gnats as blue as summer skies,
And swallowed painted butterflies?

And what would people think, if then
You laid eggs—just like any hen—
Forgot them in a windy nest,
And left the sun to do the rest?

Leave everyone—come sit with me
In trees; the things you'll hear and see!
And lead a lizard-life—I'm one!
A pocket-dragon in the sun!

JAMAICA

SNAIL

Langston Hughes (1902–1967)

Little snail,
Dreaming you go,
Weather and rose
Is all you know.

Weather and rose
Is all you see,
Drinking the dewdrop's
Mystery.

U.S.A.

LEOPARD

Edward Braithwaite (1930–)

I.

Caught therefore in this care-
ful cage of glint, rock,

water ringing the islands'
doubt, his

terror dares
not blink. A nervous tick-

like itch picks
at the corners of his

lips. The lean flanks quick
and quiver until the

tension cracks his
ribs. If he could only

strike or trigger
off his fury. But cunning

cold bars break his
rage, and stretched to strike

his stretched claws strike
no glory.

BARBADOS

ZEBU

Flavien Ranaivo (1914–)

His lips move unceasingly
But they are not swollen or worn;
His teeth are two fine rows of coral;
His horns form a circle
Which is never closed.
His eyes: two immense pearls shining in the night;
His hump is Mount-Abundance
His tail lashes the air
But is not more than half a fly-switch;
His body is a well-filled coffer
On four dry sticks.

MADAGASCAR
TRANS: *J. Reed & C. Wake*

IN AIR

Peter Clarke (contemporary)

Five gleaming crows
Are Big, black forms

Five black crows
Are
Creatures floating

38

Five black creatures
Floating
On wide-stretched air

Five gleaming forms
Are
Blackly floating

Five gleaming crows
Float blackly
On wide-stretched air.

SOUTH AFRICA

GIRAFFE

(Oral Traditional)

You who descend river by river
over the land, a fire-burnt bush,
you blue one
who looms like a far-off thorn-hill
full of people sitting together.

SOUTH AFRICA
Hottentot
TRANS: *W. H. I. Bleek*

THE EMANCIPATION OF GEORGE HECTOR

A Colored Turtle

Mari Evans (contemporary)

George-Hector
is spoiled.
formerly he stayed
well up in his
shell . . . but now
he hangs arms and legs
sprawlingly
in a most langorous fashion
head rared back
to
be
admired

he didn't use to
talk . . .
but
he does now.

U.S.A.

40

BEDBUG

(Oral Traditional)

The June-bug's got the golden wing,
The Lightning-bug the flame;
The Bedbug's got no wing at all,
But he gets there just the same.

The Pumpkin-bug's got a pumpkin smell,
The Squash-bug smells the worst;
But the perfume of that old Bedbug,
It's enough to make you burst.

When that Bedbug comes down to my house,
I take my walking cane.
Go get a pot and scald him hot!
Good-by, Miss Liza Jane!

U.S.A.

PLACES

Jamaica is a beautiful island in the West Indies surrounded by the blue-green waters of the Caribbean. Its market places are always bristling with life.

JAMAICA MARKET

Agnes Maxwell-Hall (1894–)

Honey, pepper, leaf-green limes,
Pagan fruit whose names are rhymes,
Mangoes, breadfruit, ginger-roots,
Granadillas, bamboo-shoots,
Cho-cho, ackees, tangerines,
Lemons, purple Congo-beans,
Sugar, okras, kola-nuts,
Citrons, hairy coconuts,
Fish, tobacco, native hats,
Gold bananas, woven mats,
Plantains, wild-thyme, pallid leeks,

43

Pigeons with their scarlet beaks,
Oranges and saffron yams,
Baskets, ruby guava jams,
Turtles, goat-skins, cinnamon,
Allspice, conch-shells, golden rum.
Black skins, babel—and the sun
That burns all colours into one.

JAMAICA

Ibadan is the second largest city in Nigeria. Its citizens represent over two hundred and fifty ethnic and language groups, the chief of them being Hausa, Fulani, Ibo, and Yoruba.

IBADAN

John Pepper Clark (1935–)

Ibadan,
    running splash of rust
and gold—flung and scattered
among seven hills like broken
china in the sun.

NIGERIA

Guadalupe, West Indies, is a French-speaking island with a population of about three hundred thousand.

GUADALUPE, W. I.

Nicolás Guillén (1904–)

The Negroes, labouring
by the steamer. The Arabs,
hawking their wares,
the Frenchmen, strolling, taking it easy
and the sun, burning.

In the harbour the sea
lies at rest. The air
is scorching the palm-trees . . .
I shout: "Guadalupe!" but no one answers.
The steamer departs,
ploughing the passive water to noisy spume.
Then, the Negroes
go on labouring,
the Arabs hawking their wares
the Frenchmen strolling and taking it easy
and the sun
burning.

CUBA
TRANS: *Anselm Hollo*

Barcelona is the second largest city in Spain. A seaport, it attracts people from many lands and cultures.

BARCELONA

Claude McKay (1891–1948)

In Barcelona city they dance the nights
Along the streets. The folk, erecting stands
Upon the people's pavements, come together
From pueblo, barrio, in families,
Lured by the lilting playing of the bands,
Rejoicing in the balmy summer weather,
In spreading rings they weave fine fantasies
Like rare mosaics of many-colored lights.

Kindled, it glows, the magical Sardana,
And sweeps the city in a glorious blaze.
The garrison, the sailors from the ships,
The workers join and block the city's ways,
Ripe laughter ringing from intriguing lips,
Crescending like a wonderful hosanna.

JAMAICA

46

The market place in Marrakech (Morocco) is always filled with excitement. It is a crossroads of African, Arab, and Spanish cultures and its people are of many colors.

SOUK

Ted Joans (1928–)

the market place called the souk
where many many men work by hand
on bags, skins, shoes, wood and
cloths of magnificent colors
they of the souk are magicians
when magic is applied to discarded
metal, scraps of plastic, wools and
cane-bamboo—all changed for better
by Marrakech's touch of voodoo

U.S.A.

This poem evokes a scene familiar to all in Port-au-Prince, the capital of Haiti.

EVENING IN HAITI

Emile Roumer (1903–)

A white terrace stretching far over the sea
Where flowers crush and crowd.
Branches prison you there,
At a breath roses fall, fall, like snow
And they shiver the heart with love.

The sweet soft night keeps a woman's soft touch . . .
Some Moorish fragrance it seems we breathe
Of petals brushed by the first dusk that floats.

There is peace on the sails in the port, the mists,
Peace on the wind's song too,
A luminous foam where the little waves curl
And a velvety moon in vague blue distance.

HAITI
TRANS: *Edna Worthley Underwood*

NEW YORK SKYSCRAPERS

John Mbiti (1931–)

The weak scattered rays of yellow sun
Peeped through the hazy tissues
That blanketed them with transparent wax;
And as the wrinkled rays closed the day,
Smoky chimneys of New York coughed,
Looking down in bended towers,
And vomited sad tears of dark smoke.

KENYA

SINGING WORDS

This is a classic folk Blues. Poet Langston Hughes once called them "Sad funny songs—too sad to be funny and too funny to be sad."

GO 'WAY FROM MY WINDOW
(Folk Blues)

Go 'way from my window,
Go 'way from my door;
Go 'way from my bedside,
And bother me no more,
And bother me no more.

Give me back my presents,
Give me back my ring;
Don't forget your own true love,
As long as song-birds sing,
As long as song-birds sing.

U.S.A.

Imagine a dark Creole watching one of his high-yellow brothers strutting down the street trying to out-white Whitey. You can feel him seethe with envy as he sings the words.

MISTER BANJO

(Traditional Creole Song)

See Michie Banjo there, Michie Banjo,
Struttin' down the street.
Chapeau cocked on one side, Michie Banjo,
High button shoes that squeak,
Walkin' stick a-swingin' wide, Michie Banjo,
Ev'rything's all complete.

See Michie Banjo there, Michie Banjo,
Struttin' down the street.
Di'mon' pin in his tie, Michie Banjo,
Bright yaller gloves so neat.
Trousers pleated way up high, Michie Banjo,
Ev'rything's all complete.

See Michie Banjo there, Michie Banjo,
Struttin' down the street.
Doesn't he look sweet, Michie Banjo,
Struttin' down the street!

U.S.A.

When the Reverend Martin Luther King, Jr. began his non-violent revolution, this old protest song from post-Civil War days worked its magic again for a new generation.

OH, FREEDOM

(Traditional Folk Song)

Oh, freedom! Oh, freedom!
Oh, freedom over me!
An' before I'd be a slave
I'll be buried in my grave,
An' go home to my Lord an' be free.

There'll be singin', there'll be singin',
There'll be singin' over me.
An' before I'd be a slave
I'll be buried in my grave,
An' go home to my Lord an' be free.

There'll be shoutin', there'll be shoutin',
There'll be shoutin' over me.
An' before I'd be a slave
I'll be buried in my grave,
An' go home to my Lord an' be free.

U.S.A.

LAMENT OF THE SLAVE

I am a slave born black
Black is my color
and black is my fate.
Poor me, ever suffering
this cruel pain,
even unto death.
I, Lucumi, am in bondage.
Without freedom there is no life,
so sweet little Pancha,
come on, let us dance—
For someday we Negroes
will be free!

CUBA
TRANS: *Raoul Abdul*

Although most of the people of Haiti are very poor, music and dance have always played an important part in their lives. This little lyric is self-explanatory.

SUNDAY MORNING SONG
(Folk Song)

Today oh! Oh today oh! Oh today oh!
It is Sunday morning, I settle accounts with you!
You borrowed my kerchief!
You borrowed my apron!
Today oh! Oh today oh! Oh today oh!
It is Sunday morning, I settle accounts with you!

HAITI

*This song was made up by a group of men who went to work
on a farm where they were given hardly anything to eat.*

WORK SONG

(Folk Song)

I am not coming to this man's house again,
I am not going to die for this friend.
He calls a *coumbite*, ho!
He does not have food for us,
He does not have drink for us.
If you are weary you cannot work!
I am not coming here to die again!

HAITI
TRANS: *Harold Courlander*

This is one of the favorite Calypsos of Trinidad. Calypso is a popular song form in which the singer usually improvises lyrics to suit the occasion.

CORDELIA BROWN

(Folk Song)

Oh Cordelia Brown,
What makes your head so red?
Oh Cordelia Brown,
What makes your head so red?
You sat out in the sunshine
With nothing on your head.
Oh Cordelia Brown,
That's why your head's so red.

On a moonshine night,
Oh I meet Missa Ivan.
On a moonshine night,
Oh I meet Missa Ivan.
And Missa Ivan told me
That he give 'Delia drop,
A Jamaica flop!
Because her head so red.

TRINIDAD

Saint Benedict is known as the Black Man's Saint in Brazil. During festivals in his honor, the women sing and dance this song.

GOOD SAINT BENEDICT

(Folk Song)

Good Saint Benedict,
a black man's saint,
he drinks cane juice
and gives a chesty plaint.
    Olere,
Jesus of Nazareth,
      e, e, e.

Good Saint Benedict,
once was a cook,
now he's a saint
that the true God took.
    Olere,
Jesus of Nazareth,
      e, e, e.

Good Saint Benedict,
no more crown,
what's left is a towel
from Lisbon town.
    Olere,
Jesus of Nazareth,
      e, e, e.

What saint is that,
coming in a chair?
It's good Saint Benedict
with Our Lady fair.
       Olere,
Jesus of Nazareth,
       e, e, e.

*In northeastern Brazil, songs like this one are part of a spec-
tacle that is performed at festival time. The various characters
are played by dancers.*

SEA HORSE

(Folk Song)

Sea horse, sea horse,
come forward do,
make a big bow
to the people before you.
Sea horse, sea horse,
you can come out now,
the lady of the house
has sent for you.
Sea horse, sea horse,
you dance very well,
we might even call you
darling-sweet-boy.
Sea horse, sea horse,
it's time now, it's time,
to drift away slowly
go back to your place.

BRAZIL

During the time of Mohammed, Bilal sang this Call to Prayer
from the tower of the mosque at Mecca.

CALL TO PRAYER

As sung by Bilal (c. 600)

Allah is the Most High.
I witness that there is none to worship except Allah.
I witness that Mohammed is the Apostle of Allah.
Arise to prayer! Arise to divine service!

ARAB WORLD
TRANS: *Raoul Abdul*

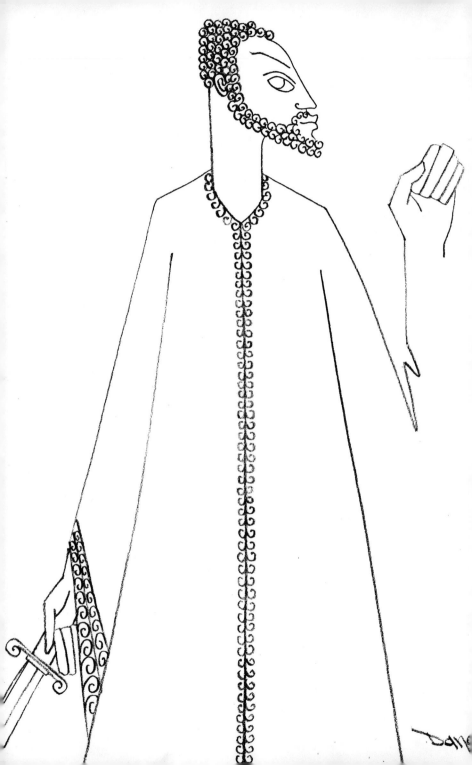

BALLADS & LEGENDS

This chilling, ghostlike tale makes good bedtime reading for young readers.

PHANTOMS OF THE STEPPE

Alexander Pushkin (1799–1837)

Clouds are swirling, clouds are straying,
    Fierce the white Snow-King's storm-might,
Dead moon's light is palely gleaming,
    Sad the heaven, sad the night.
But the sleigh goes onward, onward,
    With its little bells in line,
And my heart grows faint with terror
    At the great white snow-fields shine!

"Onward!" . . . . . "That, Master, I can not:
    See!—my steeds are wearied now,
Glued fast with the snow my eyes are,
    To go on I know not how.
No trace left here of the roadway!
    Master, tell me what to do!

Demons urge now this, now that way,
    Fastening claws on the sleigh, too!

"See! what is it white with anger
    Laughing, spitting, in my face! . . . . .
See! See!—how the frightened horses
    Toward that yawning chasm race!
Now it towers up through the darkness
    Like a pole, and now . . . See! . . . See! . . .
'Tis a wicked witch light beckoning. . . . . .
    Night again! . . . . . Oh, woe is me!

Clouds are whirling, clouds are straying,
    Fierce the white Snow-King's storm-might,
Dead moon's light is palely gleaming,
    Sad the heaven, sad the night.
Suddenly they pause—the horses,
    Silent, too, the little bell . . .
See! what's crouching on the earth there?
    "Master . . . wolves?" . . . . . "I can not tell."

Hark!—the wind now, wailing, moaning!
    The span scents danger, crouches low . . .
There! . . . It's coming! . . . How its eyes gleam!
    Onward! . . . . . fast as you can go!"
Hardly can we hold the horses,
    And the bells shrill loud and clear,
Just see with what scornful gestures
    That wild phantom host draws near!

64

See that endless, pale procession,
      Countless, formless, fleet as mind,
Circling, whirling, in their flight here,
      Like dry leaves in autumn wind!
Now a silence, fearful, deadly!
      Now shrill sounds of grief and woe. . . . .
Is it wedding dance-song medley,
      Or a death-march sad and slow?

Clouds are whirling, clouds are straying,
      Fierce the white Snow-King's storm-might,
Dead moon's light is palely gleaming
      Sad the heavens, sad the night.
Crowd on crowd of phantoms drifting
      Upward, upward, out of sight. . . . .
And their wailing and their moaning
      Chill my heart with fear to-night!

RUSSIA
TRANS: *Edna Worthley Underwood*

Reports of the colorful adventures of the Arab poet-warrior-hero Antar have been passed down through so many generations that it is now hard to tell fact from fiction. In this short excerpt from over thirty-two volumes, I have tried to capture the spirit of his personality.

THE ROMANCE OF ANTAR

An Excerpt
Antar (d. 600)

(Antar is about to go into battle with a foe. They rush together like two whirlwinds. Swords flash. Valiant blows are struck; yet neither at first gains victory. Then, a new tide rises in Antar, and even as he fights, he begins to compose a poem):

"I am Antar!" he chants.

"I am he whose might is uncontrollable in battle—
the valiant lion of the cavern.
I plunge into the flames of war with the gleaming
scimitar, and I feed them with the stabbing
lance."

(Here, his foe strikes him a strong blow, but our hero recovers and continues):

"I drive back the horses on their haunches from my
lofty seat on Abjer of the thin flanks.

I strike with the blade of my sword Dhami, at whose
    edge flow the waves of death over the enemy."

(Quite angered, his foe rushes into silence both the words
and blows of our hero. But Antar continues):

"My sword is my father, and the spear in my hand is
    my father's brother.
I am the son of my day on the heights of the desert.
Verily, night may be my complexion, but day is my
    emblem.
The sun itself is brother to Antar the Unconquerable!"

(Our hero drives a sword into his foe and says):

"This day shall you taste the bitterness of death!"

ARAB WORLD
Adapted by *Raoul Abdul*

CHRISTMAS

GO TELL IT ON THE MOUNTAIN

(Traditional Spiritual)

Go tell it on the mountain,
Over the hills and everywhere;
Go tell it on the mountain,
That Jesus Christ is born.

> When I was a seeker,
> I sought both night and day,
> I asked the Lord to help me,
> And he showed me the way.

> He made me a watchman
> Upon a city wall,
> And if I am a Christian,
> I am the least of all.

Go tell it on the mountain,
Over the hills and everywhere;
Go tell it on the mountain,
That Jesus Christ is born.

U.S.A.

CONCEPTION

Waring Cuney (1906–)

Jesus' mother never had no man,
God came to her one day an' said,
"Mary, chile, kiss ma han'."

U.S.A.

CHRISTUS NATUS EST

Countee Cullen (1903–1946)

In Bethlehem
On Christmas morn,
The lowly gem
Of love was born.
Hosannah! *Christus natus est.*

Bright in her crown
Of fiery star,
Judea's town
Shone from afar:
Hosannah! *Christus natus est.*

While beasts in stall,
On bended knee,
Did carol all
Most joyously:
Hosannah! *Christus natus est.*

For bird and beast
He did not come,
But for the least
Of mortal scum.
Hosannah! *Christus natus est.*

Who lies in ditch?
Who begs his bread?
Who has no stitch
Hosannah! *Christus natus est.*

Who wakes to weep,
Lies down to mourn?
Who in his sleep
Withdraws from scorn?
Hosannah! *Christus natus est.*

Ye outraged dust,
On field and plain,
To feed the lust
Of madmen slain:
Hosannah! *Christus natus est.*

The manger still
Outshines the throne;
Christ must and will
Come to his own.
Hosannah! *Christus natus est.*

U.S.A.

71

CONFESSION STONE

A Song Cycle Sung by Mary about Jesus

Owen Dodson (1914–)

I.

Oh my boy: Jesus,
My first and only son,
Rock on my breast
My first and only one.
My first and only son.
Oh my Jesus:
My first and only one:
Born of God and born
    near His sun
Bright boy: My only one:
Oh my Jesus
Rest on my breast
My first and only son:
Oh my boy Jesus: rest.
Shushhh, you need the rest.

U.S.A.

72

SHEPHERD'S SONG AT CHRISTMAS

Langston Hughes (1902–1967)

Look there at the star!
I, among the least,
Will arise and take
A journey to the East.
*But what shall I bring
As a present for the King?
What shall I bring to the Manger?*

I will bring a song,
A song that I will sing,
In the Manger.

Watch out for my flocks,
Do not let them stray.
I am going on a journey
Far, far away.
*But what shall I bring
As a present for the Child?
What shall I bring to the Manger?*

I will bring a lamb,
Gentle, meek, and mild,
A lamb for the Child
In the Manger.

I'm just a shepherd boy,
Very poor I am—
But I know there is
A King in Bethlehem.
What shall I bring
As a present just for Him?
What shall I bring to the Manger?

I will bring my heart
And give my heart to Him.
I will bring my heart
To the Manger.

U.S.A.

THE THREE KINGS

Rubén Darío (1867–1916)

"I am Gaspar. I have brought frankincense,
and I have come here to say that life is good.
That God exists. That love is everything.
I know it is so because of the heavenly star."

"I am Melchior. I have brought fragrant myrrh.
Yes, God exists. He is the light of day.
The white flower is rooted in the mud,
and all delights are tinged with melancholy."

"I am Balthasar. I have brought gold.
I assure you, God exists. He is great and strong.
I know it is so because of the perfect star
that shines so brightly in Death's diadem."

"Gaspar, Melchior, Balthasar: be still.
Love has triumphed, and bids you to its feast.
Christ, reborn, turns chaos into light,
and on His brow He wears the Crown of Life."

NICARAGUA
TRANS: *Lysander Kemp*

GIFT

Carol Freeman (1941–)

christmas morning i
got up before the others and
ran
naked across the plank
floor into the front
room to see grandmama
sewing a new
button on my last year
ragdoll.

U.S.A.

KID STUFF

Frank Horne (1899–)

The wise guys
tell me
that Christmas
is Kid Stuff . . .
Maybe they've got
something there—
Two thousand years ago
three wise guys
chased a star
across a continent
to bring
frankincense and myrrh
to a Kid
born in a manger
with an idea in his head . . .

And as the bombs
crash
all over the world
today
the real wise guys
know
that we've all
got to go chasing stars
again
in the hope

that we can get back
some of that
Kid Stuff
born two thousand years ago.

U.S.A.

HEROES

*This powerful protest song was used by early black leaders
to make the slaves rise up against their oppressors.*

GO DOWN, MOSES

(Traditional Folk Song)

When Israel was in Egyp' Lan',
Let my people go,
Oppressed so hard they could not stan',
Let my people go.

Go down, Moses,
Way down in Egyp' Lan',
Tell ole Pharaoh
To let my people go.

Thus spoke the Lord, bold Moses said,
Let my people go,
If not I'll smit your first-born dead,
Let my people go.

U.S.A.

The idea of a little boy being able to outwit a giant caught the imagination of the slaves of our American South and led to the creation of this favorite Spiritual.

LITTLE DAVID

(Traditional Spiritual)

Little David play on your harp,
Hallelu, hallelu,
Little David play on your harp,
Hallelu.

David was a shepherd boy,
He killed Goliath,
An' he shouted for joy.

Now, Joshua was the son of Nun,
He never stop,
'Till his work was done.

Little David play on your harp,
Hallelu, hallelu,
Little David play on your harp,
Hallelu.

U.S.A.

The legend of John Henry, the steel driller of West Virginia, has been celebrated in many folk songs. A contest was arranged by two companies in Big Bend Tunnel—John Henry against a steam drill.

JOHN HENRY

(Traditional Ballad)

John Henry said to his captain,
"A man ain't nothing but a man.
An' before I'll let your steam drill beat me down,
Die with the hammer in my hand, Lawd, Lawd!
Die with the hammer in my hand."

John Henry got a thirty pound hammer,
Beside the steam drill he did stand.
He beat that steam drill three inches down,
An' died with his hammer in his hand, Lawd, Lawd!
Died with his hammer in his hand.

John Henry had a pretty little boy,
Sittin' in the palm of his hand.
He hugged and kissed him an' bid him farewell,
"Oh son, do the best you can, Lawd, Lawd!
Son, do the best you can."

They took John Henry to the graveyard
An' they buried him in the sand,
An' ev'ry locomotive come roarin' by
Says, "Dere lays a steel-drivin' man, Lawd, Lawd!
Dere lays a steel-drivin' man."

U.S.A.

Henri Christophe was the last of three great Haitian heroes.
He erected the famous Citadel on the summit of La Ferrière,
a mountain overlooking Milot and the harbor of Le Cap.

CHRISTOPHE

Russell Atkins (1926–)

Upstood upstaffed

             passing sinuously away over an airy
            arch
  streaming where all th' lustres
  streaming
        sinuously shone
  bright
     where more sky
Upstood upstaffed

          th' sumptuously ready
  flags full—
  (th' shaded soothed an' blowing softly
  th' underlings smoothly
  with horses
        wavering with winds
  tangling with manly manners
              thick
  gathering th' steeds)
         that
  forthwith
  up up
  Christophe
  appearing in th' imminent
  an' th' passion overjoying the hour

unfolded
    flaming
Highly th' imperial sign
shone in his glory!

U.S.A.

Frederick Douglass played an extraordinary role in American history. Born a slave, he became a leader of the abolitionist movement and counsel to President Abraham Lincoln.

FREDERICK DOUGLASS

Robert Hayden (1913–)

When it is finally ours, this freedom, this liberty,
   this beautiful
and terrible thing, needful to man as air,
usable as earth; when it belongs at last to all,
when it is truly instinct, brain matter, diastole, systole,
reflex action; when it is finally won; when it is more
than the gaudy mumbo jumbo of politicians:
this man, this Douglass, this former slave, this Negro
beaten to his knees, exiled, visioning a world
where none is lonely, none hunted, alien,
this man, superb in love and logic, this man
shall be remembered. Oh, not with statues' rhetoric,
not with legends and poems and wreaths of bronze alone,
but with the lives grown out of his life, the lives
fleshing his dream of the beautiful, needful thing.

U.S.A.

Booker T. Washington and W. E. B. DuBois were both famous black leaders. They were constantly at variance as to how each should achieve his goal.

BOOKER T. AND W. E. B.

Dudley Randall (1914–)

"It seems to me," said Booker T.,
"It shows a mighty lot of cheek
To study chemistry and Greek
When Mister Charlie needs a hand
To hoe the cotton on his land,
And when Miss Ann looks for a cook,
Why stick your nose inside a book?"

"I don't agree," said W. E. B.,
"If I should have the drive to seek
Knowledge of chemistry or Greek,
I'll do it. Charles and Miss can look
Another place for hand or cook.
Some men rejoice in skill of hand,
And some in cultivating land,
But there are others who maintain
The right to cultivate the brain."

"It seems to me," said Booker T.,
"That all you folks have missed the boat
Who shout about the right to vote,
And spend vain days and sleepless nights
In uproar over civil rights.
Just keep your mouths shut, do not grouse,
But work, and save, and buy a house."

"I don't agree," said W. E. B.,
"For what can property avail
If dignity and justice fail.
Unless you help to make the laws,
They'll steal your house with trumped-up clause.
A rope's as tight, a fire as hot,
No matter how much cash you've got.
Speak soft, and try your little plan,
But as for me, I'll be a man."

"It seems to me," said Booker T.—

"I don't agree,"
Said W. E. B.

U.S.A.

85

One day in 1955 in Montgomery, Alabama, a seamstress, Mrs. Rosa Parks, was rudely ordered by a bus driver to give up her seat to a white man and move to the back of the bus. Her refusal caused her to be arrested. This incident inspired the Reverend Martin Luther King, Jr., to organize a massive bus boycott which focused worldwide attention on the great leader of the nonviolent revolution.

IT HAPPENED IN MONTGOMERY

Phil W. Petrie (1937–)

For Rosa Parks

Then he slammed on the brakes—
Turned around and grumbled.

But she was tired that day.
Weariness was in her bones.
And so the thing she's done yesterday,
And yesteryear,
On her workdays,
Churchdays,
Nothing-to-do-guess-I'll-go-and-visit Sister Annie
Days—

She felt she'd never do again.

And he growled once more.

So she said:
No sir . . . I'm stayin' right here.

And he gruffly grabbed her,
Pulled and pushed her—
Then sharply shoved her through the doors.

The news slushed through the littered streets—
Slipped into the crowded churches,
Slimmered onto the unmagnolied side of town
While the men talked and talked and talked.

She—
Who was tired that day,
Cried and sobbed that she was glad she'd done it,
That her soul was satisfied.

That Lord knows,
A little walkin' never hurt anybody;

That in one of those unplanned, unexpected,
Unadorned moments—
A weary woman turned the page of History.

U.S.A.

Malcolm X, who was assassinated at the peak of his career, was the leader of the black nationalist movement. His autobiography is one of the most widely read books by black American youth.

MALCOLM X

Gwendolyn Brooks (1917–)

Original.
Ragged-round.
Rich-robust.

He had the hawk-man's eyes.
We gasped. We saw the maleness.
The maleness raking out and making guttural the air
and pushing us to walls.

And in a soft and fundamental hour
a sorcery devout and vertical
beguiled the world.

He opened us—
who was a key,

who was a man.

U.S.A.

Satchell Paige is a legend in the baseball world. He played until he was well into his fifties and is reputed to have said that that he would die on the mound—winding up for the pitch.

TO SATCH

Samuel Allen (1917–)

Sometimes I feel like I will *never* stop
Just go on forever
Till one fine mornin'
I'm gonna reach up and grab me a handfulla stars
Swing out my long lean leg
And whip three hot strikes burnin' down the heavens
And look over at God and say,
How about that!

U.S.A.

Jack Johnson, one of the greatest fighters in the history of American boxing, has recently been the subject of a play, The Great White Hope. *He lived between 1876–1946.*

MY LORD, WHAT A MORNING

Waring Cuney (1906–)

Oh, my Lord
What a morning,
Oh, my Lord,
What a feeling,
When Jack Johnson
Turned Jim Jeffries'
Snow-white face
Up to the ceiling.
Yes, my Lord,
Fighting is wrong,
But what an uppercut.
Oh, my Lord,
What a morning.
Oh, my Lord
What a feeling,
When Jack Johnson
Turned Jim Jeffries'
Lily-white face
Up to the ceiling.
Oh, my Lord
What a morning,
Oh, my Lord

Take care of Jack.
Keep him, Lord
As you made him,
Big, and strong, and black.

U.S.A.

LIKE IT IS

ONE THOUSAND NINE HUNDRED
& SIXTY-EIGHT WINTERS

Jaci Earley (contemporary)

Got up this morning
Feeling good & black
Thinking black thoughts
Did black things
Played all my black records
And minded my own black business
Put on my best black clothes
Walked out my black door
And, Lord have mercy: white snow!

U.S.A.

INCIDENT

Countee Cullen (1903–1946)

Once riding in old Baltimore,
    Heart-filled, head-filled with glee,
I saw a Baltimorean
    Keep looking straight at me.

Now I was eight and very small,
    And he was no whit bigger,
And so I smiled, but he poked out
    His tongue, and called me, "Nigger."

I saw the whole of Baltimore
    from May until December;
Of all the things that happened there
    That's all that I remember.

U.S.A.

MERRY-GO-ROUND

Langston Hughes (1902–1967)

(Colored Child at Carnival)

    Where is the Jim Crow section
    On this merry-go-round,
    Mister, 'cause I want to ride?

94

Down South where I come from
White and colored
Can't sit side by side
Down South on the train
There's a Jim Crow car.
On the bus we're put in the back—
But there ain't no back
To a merry-go-round!
Where's the horse
For a kid that's black?

U.S.A.

Some people of African-Spanish origin do not wish to identify with their darker brothers. They try to conceal the fact that somewhere in the background is a black grandmother.

LAST NIGHT SOMEBODY CALLED ME DARKY

Nicolás Guillén (1904–)

Last night somebody called me darky
jes' to make me fight,
but the one who said it to me
is a darky, too, all right.

Can't fool me, that white face of yours
'cause I know who your grandma is.

Call her out the kitchen,
Call her out the kitchen,
Mama Inez.
Mama Inez, you know all about it.
Mama Inez, I know, too.
Mama Inez calls you grandson,
Mama Inez.

CUBA
TRANS: *Langston Hughes*

WE REAL COOL

Gwendolyn Brooks (1917–)

The Pool Players.
Seven at the Golden Shovel.

We real cool. We
Left school. We

Lurk late. We
Strike straight. We

Sing sin. We
Thin gin. We

Jazz June. We
Die soon.

U.S.A.

MOTHER TO SON

Langston Hughes (1902–1967)

Well, son, I'll tell you:
Life for me ain't been no crystal stair.
It's had tacks in it,
And splinters,
And boards torn up,
And places with no carpet on the floor—
Bare.
But all the time
I'se been a-climbin' on,
And reachin' landin's,
And turnin' corners,
And sometimes goin' in the dark
Where there ain't been no light.
So boy, don't you turn back.
Don't you set down on the steps
'Cause you finds it's kinder hard.
Don't you fall now—
For I'se still goin', honey,
I'se still climbin',
And life for me ain't been no crystal stair.

U.S.A.

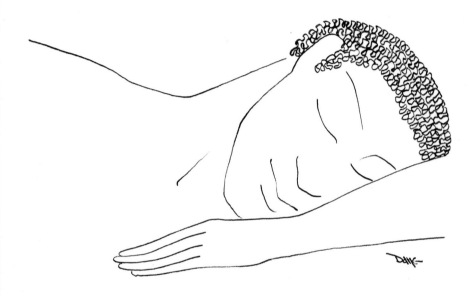

NIGHT

NIGHT SONG

Langston Hughes (1902–1967)

In the dark
Before the tall
Moon came,
Little short
Dusk
Was walking
Along.

In the dark
Before the tall
Moon came,
Little short
Dusk
Was singing
A song.

In the dark
Before the tall
Moon came,
A lady named
Day
Fainted away
In the
Dark.

U.S.A.

LITTLE BROWN BABY

Paul Laurence Dunbar (1872–1906)

Little brown baby wif spa'klin' eyes,
  Come to yo' pappy an' set on his knee.
What you been doin', suh—makin' san' pies?
  Look at dat bib—you's ez du'ty ez me.
Look at dat moug—dat's merlasses, I bet;
  Come hyeah, Maria, an' wipe off his han's.
Bees gwine to ketch you an' eat you up yit,
  Bein' so sticky an' sweet—goodness lan's!

Little brown baby wif spa'klin' eyes,
  Who's pappy's darlin' an' who's pappy's chile?
Who is it all de day nevah once tries
  Fu' to be cross, er once loses dat smile?
Whah did you git dem teef? My, you's a scamp!
  What did dat dimple come f'om in yo' chin?

Pappy do' know you—I b'lieves you's a tramp;
    Mammy, dis hyeah's some ol' straggler got in!

Let's th'ow him outen de do' in de san',
    We do' want stragglers a-layin' 'roun' hyeah;
Let's gin him 'way to de big buggah-man;
    I know he's hidin' erroun' hyeah right neah.
Buggah-man, buggah-man, come in de do',
    Hyeah's a bad boy you kin have fu' to eat.
Mammy an' pappy do' want him no mo',
    Swaller him down f'om his haid to his feet!

Dah, now, I t'ought dat you'd hug me up close.
    Go back, ol' buggah, you sha'n't have dis boy.
He ain't no tramp, ner no straggler, of co'se;
    He's pappy's pa'dner an' playmate an' joy.
Come to you' pallet now—go to yo' res';
    Wisht you could allus know ease an' cleah skies:
Wisht you could stay jes' a chile on my breas'—
    Little brown baby wif spa'klin' eyes!

U.S.A.

THE SWEETEST THING

(Traditional)

There is in this world something
that surpasses all other things
in sweetness.
It is sweeter than honey
it is sweeter than salt
it is sweeter than sugar
it is sweeter than all
existing things.
This thing is sleep.
When you are conquered by sleep
nothing can ever prevent you
nothing can stop you from sleeping.
When you are conquered by sleep
and numerous millions arrive
millions arrive to disturb you
millions will find you asleep.

GUINEA
TRANS: *Ulli Beier*

FOUR GLIMPSES OF NIGHT

Frank Marshall Davis (1905–)

III.

Peddling
From door to door
Night sells
Black bags of peppermint stars
Heaping cones of vanilla moon
Until
His wares are gone
Then shuffles homeward
Jingling the gray coins
Of daybreak.

U.S.A.

TOMORROWS

THIS MORNING

Jay Wright (1935–)

This morning I threw the windows
of my room open, the light burst
in like crystal gauze and I hung
it on my wall to frame.
And here I am watching it take possession
of my room, watching the obscure love
match of light and shadow—of cold and warmth.
It is a matter of finding some room
with shadows to embrace, open. Now
the light has settled in, I don't think
I shall ever close my windows again.

U.S.A.

POEM OF THE FUTURE CITIZEN

José Craveirinha (1922–)

I came from somewhere
from a Nation which does not yet exist.
I came and I am here!

Not I alone was born
nor you nor any other . . .
but brothers.

I have love to give in handfuls.
Love of what I am
and nothing more.

I have a heart
and cries which are not mine alone
I come from a country which does not yet exist.

Ah! I have love in plenty to give
of what I am.
I!
A man among many
citizen of a Nation which has yet to exist.

MOZAMBIQUE
TRANS: *Philippa Rumsey*

In order to appreciate fully the sentiment of this poem, it is important to know that the poet is a citizen of the Union of South Africa where separation of the races is maintained by brute force.

WHERE THE RAINBOW ENDS

Richard Rive (1931–)

Where the rainbow ends
There's going to be a place, brother,
Where the world can sing all sorts of songs,
And we're going to sing together, brother,
You and I, though you're white and I'm not.
It's going to be a sad song, brother,
Because we don't know the tune,
And it's a difficult tune to learn.
But we can learn, brother, you and I.
There's no such tune as a black tune.
There's no such tune as a white tune.
There's only music, brother,
And it's music we're going to sing
Where the rainbow ends.

SOUTH AFRICA

EPILOGUE

FOR A POET

Countee Cullen (1903–1946)

I have wrapped my dreams in a silken cloth,
And laid them away in a box of gold;
Where long will cling the lips of the moth,
I have wrapped my dreams in a silken cloth;
I hide no hate; I am not even wroth
Who found earth's breath so keen and cold;
I have wrapped my dreams in a silken cloth,
And laid them away in a box of gold.

U.S.A.

ABOUT THE POETS

PHARAOH AKHENATON (c. 1350 B.C.) was one of the first of the early kings to advocate the worship of one God. Since he thought that the Sun was the Creator he composed his lovely *Hymn to the Sun*, which has come down to us through the ages. (EGYPT) (Page 3)

SAMUEL ALLEN (1917–) attended Fisk University, Harvard Law School, New York University, and the Sorbonne in Paris. As a poet he first came to international attention through his book *Ivory Tusks*, which was published in Heidelberg, Germany. He is now represented in every major anthology of black poetry. (U.S.A.) (Page 89)

ANTAR (c. 600) was a great Arab warrior-poet. Through the years, his deeds have been so romanticized that it is hard to tell which is fact or fiction. His famous *Ode* is written in letters of gold in the Temple at Mecca. (ARABIA) (Page 66)

RUSSELL ATKINS (1926–) is a musician and poet. His poems have appeared in magazines since the 1940s, and his recently published volumes include *Phenomena* (1963), *Objects* (1963), and *Heretofore* (1968). (U.S.A.) (Page 82)

ERNEST ATTAH (contemporary) is a graduate of Harvard University. His poetry has appeared in *New African Literature and the Arts I.* (NIGERIA) (Page 24)

EDWARD BRAITHWAITE (1930–) has taught at the University of the West Indies in Jamaica and is author of several books of poetry including *Rights of Passage* and *Islands*. (BARBADOS) (Pages 13, 36)

BILAL (c. 600) was the first man appointed to chant the Muslim *Call to Prayer*. His close association with the Prophet Mohammed caused him to be named successor, but he yielded in favor of the great General Abu Bekr. (ARABIA) (Page 61)

GWENDOLYN BROOKS (1917–) won a Pulitzer Prize for her poetry, as well as being chosen Poet Laureate of the State of Illinois. Her collections include *Annie Allen, Bronzeville Boys and Girls, The Bean Eaters, Selected Poems, In the Mecca,* and others. She has encouraged many young people to write poetry by personally giving awards to those of special talent. (U.S.A.) (Pages 28, 88, 96)

JOHN PEPPER CLARK (1935–) was educated at Ibadan University and also at Princeton. His poetry has been widely published throughout the English-speaking world. (NIGERIA) (Page 44)

PETER CLARKE (contemporary) is equally talented as painter and poet. His paintings have been exhibited at the National Gallery in South Africa, and his poems appear in such anthologies as *Poems of Black Africa.* (SOUTH AFRICA) (Pages 10, 38)

JOSÉ CRAVEIRINHA (1922–) is a journalist and poet. His poems appear in such anthologies as *Modern Poetry from Africa* (MOZAMBIQUE) (Page 106)

COUNTEE CULLEN (1903–1946), who won great recognition as a poet, also found time to teach in the New York Public Schools. His interest in young people led to the publication of *The Lost Zoo* and *My Nine Lives and How I Lost Them.* His volumes of poetry include *Color, Copper Sun, The Ballad of the Brown Girl, The Black Christ, The Medea and Some Poems, On These I Stand,* and the classic anthology *Caroling Dusk.* (U.S.A.) (Pages 27, 28, 70, 94, 109)

WARING CUNEY (1906–) is the author of the poem *No Images,* which is one of the most widely published works of an

American black poet. He attended schools in Washington, D.C., Pennsylvania, Boston, and Rome where he divided his interests between music and poetry. (U.S.A.) (Pages 70, 90)

PIERRE DALCOUR (19th century) was a Creole from New Orleans. His charming verses appear in French in the anthology *Les Cenelles*, compiled by Armand Lanusse in 1845. (U.S.A.) (Page 24)

RUBÉN DARÍO (1867–1916), with his combination of Spanish-Indian-African blood, led a movement which revitalized Spanish literature. His *Selected Poems* have been published in an excellent English translation by Lysander Kemp. (NICARAGUA) (Page 74)

FRANK MARSHALL DAVIS (1905–) helped found the great black newspaper *Atlanta Daily World*. His poetry won him a Rosenwald Fellowship and he is author of several books of poems including *Black Man's Verse, I Am the American Negro*, and *47th Street*. (U.S.A.) (Page 103)

OWEN DODSON (1914–) was for many years Chairman of the Drama Department of Howard University. He is now Artistic Consultant at the Harlem School of the Arts Community Theatre. His poetry has been included in over thirty-five anthologies, and he has a volume entitled *Powerful Long Ladder* in print since 1946. (U.S.A.) (Page 72)

ABU DOLAMA (d. 778) was an Abyssinian black who was court jester to the Caliphs Mansur and Mahdi. His biting humour frequently aroused the ire of those he made fun of, but always amused them. (ARABIA) (Page 33)

PAUL LAURENCE DUNBAR (1872–1906) was one of the earliest black American poets to gain wide recognition. He lived to see many of his volumes of poetry in print, all of which have been collected in *Complete Poems*. (U.S.A.) (Pages 21, 33, 100)

RAY DUREM (1915–1963) was a member of the International Brigade during the Spanish Civil War. His poems have appeared in many anthologies, including *The Poetry of the Negro*. (U.S.A.) (Page 32)

JACI EARLEY (contemporary) has had poetry published in *Liberator, Revolt, Journal of Black Poetry, Black Culture Weekly, Soulscript,* and elsewhere. (U.S.A.) (Page 93)

JAMES A. EMANUEL (1921–) has a Ph.D. from Columbia University. He is co-editor of *Dark Symphony,* an anthology of Negro literature in America, and his poems have appeared on the pages of *The New York Times* and in anthologies. (U.S.A.) (Page 17)

MARI EVANS (contemporary) has had her poems published in over thirty anthologies. Her recent volume *I am a Black Woman* has been highly acclaimed. (U.S.A.) (Page 40)

CAROL FREEMAN (1941–) attended Oakland City College and the University of California. Her poems appear in *3000 Years of Black Poetry, Black Fire,* and elsewhere (U.S.A.) (Page 75)

HERBERT D. GREGGS (1931–) is an actor-playwright-lyricist. He has appeared at Cleveland's Karamu Theatre, off-Broadway, and elsewhere and has written a musical *The Ballad of Riverboat Town.* (U.S.A.) (Page 16)

NICOLÁS GUILLÉN (1904–) is the leader of the Afro-Cuban school of poetry. His *Cuba Libre,* with its excellent English translation by Ben F. Carruthers and Langston Hughes, is now a collector's item. (CUBA) (Pages 4, 14, 45, 95)

ROBERT HAYDEN (1913–) won the Grand Prize for Poetry at the *First World Festival of Negro Arts* at Dakar, Senegal. Among his published works are *Heart-Shape in the Dust, A Ballad of Remembrance, Selected Poems,* and an anthology, *Kalaidescope.* (U.S.A.) (Page 83)

FRANK HORNE (1899–) is a leading authority on housing and he has held many important government posts. Poetry writing has always remained one of his main interests and his works have been collected in the recently published volume *Haverstraw*. (U.S.A.) (Page 76)

LANGSTON HUGHES (1902–1967) is America's most famous black writer. Over thirty of his books have been published, many of which were especially for young people. These include *The Dream Keeper, Famous American Negroes, Famous Negro Music Makers, Famous American Negro Heroes, First Book of Negroes, First Book of Jazz, First Book of Rhythms,* and *First Book of the West Indies*. (U.S.A.) (Pages 4, 9, 21, 36, 73, 94, 97, 99)

ZORA NEALE HURSTON (1903–1960) captured on paper many of the imaginative folk sermons preached in country churches. Her published works include *Jonah's Gourd Vine, Mules and Men, Their Eyes Were Watching God, Moses, Man of the Mountain,* and *Seraph on the Suwannee*. (U.S.A.) (Pages 1, 7)

TED JOANS (1928–) was born on a riverboat near Cairo, Illinois. Poet, painter, and jazz musician, he has traveled throughout the world. Among his published works are *Black Pow-Wow* and *Afrodisia*. (U.S.A.) (Page 47)

ARMAND LANUSSE (1812–1867) was a member of a distinguished social group in New Orleans known as Free Men of Color. He compiled a remarkable little volume of French Creole poetry entitled *Les Cenelles* (Holly-Berries). (U.S.A.) (Page 30)

MATEI MARKWEI (contemporary) is an ordained minister who attended Lincoln University, Pennsylvania, and Yale University. (GHANA) (Page 20)

AGNES MAXWELL-HALL (1894–) was educated in London, Boston, and New York. Her poetry appears in the anthologies *3000 Years of Black Poetry* and *The Poetry of the Negro*. (JAMAICA) (Pages 35, 43)

John Mbiti (1931–) has a doctorate from Westminister College in Cambridge, England. He has taught religious subjects at Makerere University College in Uganda and his poetry appears in *Modern Poetry from Africa* and elsewhere. (kenya) (Page 49)

Claude McKay (1891–1948) gained worldwide fame when Sir Winston Churchill read his sonnet *If We Must Die* in the British House of Commons. He wrote poetry, novels, autobiographies, and sociological studies. His volumes of poetry include *Songs of Jamaica, Spring in New Hampshire, Harlem Shadows,* and *Selected Poems.* (jamaica) (Page 46)

Faarah Nuur (d. 1930) led his clan in a struggle for independence and achieved a spectacular victory against overwhelming odds. His poetry has been made available in English translation in *Somali Poetry,* edited by B. W. Andrzejewski and I. M. Lewis. (somaliland) (Page 29)

Christopher Okigbo (1932–67) was active in Nigerian literary circles following his graduation from University College at Ibadan. Born in the Ibo country of Eastern Nigeria, he was killed in action with the Biafran Army. His published volumes of poetry include *Heavensgate* and *The Limits and Other Poems.* (nigeria) (Page 6)

Phil W. Petrie (1937–) is a graduate of Tennessee State University where his special interests were poetry writing, political science, and English. A senior editor at William Morrow & Co., his poetry appears in several anthologies. (u.s.a.) (Page 86)

Alexander Pushkin (1799–1837) is known as the father of Russian literature. He was descended on his father's side from an old aristocratic Russian family and on his mother's side from an Ethiopian General Hannibal. Many of his works have been translated into English and widely published. (russia) (Page 63)

IBN QUZMAN (d. 1160) was a famous Moorish poet. (MOORISH SPAIN) (Page 31)

FLAVIEN RANAIVO (1914–) is the son of a governor of Arivonimamo. He has spent much time wandering through the countryside and his poetry is influenced by song and ballad forms. (MADAGASCAR) (Page 38)

DUDLEY RANDALL (1914–) created Broadside Press in Detroit, through which he has given many fine black poets the opportunity to have their works published in beautiful editions. His own poetry is published in many anthologies, including *Kalaidescope*. (U.S.A.) (Page 84)

RICHARD RIVE (1931–) has been widely published in German and Scandinavian countries and in such anthologies as *Poems from Black Africa*. (SOUTH AFRICA) (Page 107)

EMILE ROUMER (1903–) was one of the founders of an important Haitian poetry journal. Educated in France, he returned to his land to practice law and publish two books of poetry. English translations of his works appear in *The Poets of Haiti*. (HAITI) (Page 48)

IBN SHARAF (d. 1068) was a Moorish Poet. (ARABIC WORLD) (Page 32)

SAUNDRA SHARP (contemporary) is a poet and actress. She was seen in the film *The Learning Tree* and on stage in *Hello, Dolly, To Be Young, Gifted, and Black, Black Quartet,* and *Black Girl*. Her poetry appears in *We Speak as Liberators: Young Black Poets Speak*, and elsewhere. (U.S.A.) (Page 5)

JAY WRIGHT (1935–) attended the University of New Mexico, the University of California at Berkeley, Union Theological Seminary in New York, and Rutgers University. His poems have appeared in magazines and anthologies, including *New Negro Poets: USA*. (U.S.A.) (Page 105)

ABOUT THE EDITOR

RAOUL ABDUL divides his time between writing and singing. Co-editor with Alan Lomax of *3000 Years of Black Poetry*, he was long time assistant to the late Langston Hughes. His interest in black poetry and folk-song led him to create a program *The Negro Speaks of Rivers* which played ten performances at the *1962 Vienna Festival*, opened *Brotherhood Week* in 1962 (Nuremberg, Germany), toured three years in colleges and universities (U.S.A.) and was shown three times on television.

ABOUT THE ARTIST

DANE BURR was formerly on the staff of Cleveland's famous interracial center Karamu House. His ceramic sculptures, *Dane Originals*, are on exhibit and for sale at such institutions as National Audubon Society (New York), Museum of Arts and Sciences (Boston), City Art Museum (St. Louis) and the Rochester Museum of Arts and Sciences (Rochester, N. Y.).